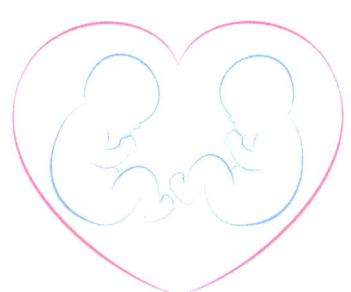

A Tale of Two Souls

A Tale of Two Souls

SHAI HAR-EL

Homestead Lighthouse Press
Grants Pass, Oregon

A Tale of Two Souls Copyright © 2022 by Shai Har-El. All rights reserved. Any unauthorized reprint or use of this material is prohibited. No part of this book may be reproduced or transmitted in any form or by any means, electronic or mechanical, including photocopying, recording, or by any information storage and retrieval system without prior written permission of the publisher.

ISBN 978-1-950475-21-6

Library of Congress Control Number: 2022930404

The pictures throughout the book were taken by the author in the Chicago Botanic Garden, Glencoe, IL.

Cover illustration 50621538 © Peter Hermes Furian
Book and cover design by Ray Rhamey

Homestead Lighthouse Press
1668 NE Foothill Boulevard
Unit A
Grants Pass, OR 97526
www.homesteadlighthousepress.com

Distributed by Homestead Lighthouse Press, Daedalus Distribution, Amazon.com, Barnes & Noble

Homestead Lighthouse Press gratefully acknowledges the generous support of its readers and patrons.

I dedicate this book
to my incredible grandchildren:
Hannah
Liam
Mia
Uma
Eden
Clara
Sivan
Elijah
Nomi
Naama
Reut

who keep me young and joyful.
I am grateful to have you in my life.

אֱלֹהַי. נְשָׁמָה שֶׁנָּתַתָּ בִּי טְהוֹרָה הִיא. אַתָּה בְרָאתָהּ, אַתָּה יְצַרְתָּהּ, אַתָּה נְפַחְתָּהּ בִּי, וְאַתָּה מְשַׁמְּרָהּ בְּקִרְבִּי, וְאַתָּה עָתִיד לִטְּלָהּ מִמֶּנִּי, וּלְהַחֲזִירָהּ בִּי לֶעָתִיד לָבוֹא: כָּל זְמַן שֶׁהַנְּשָׁמָה בְקִרְבִּי, מוֹדֶה אֲנִי לְפָנֶיךָ יְיָ אֱלֹהַי וֵאלֹהֵי אֲבוֹתַי, רִבּוֹן כָּל הַמַּעֲשִׂים, אֲדוֹן כָּל הַנְּשָׁמוֹת. בָּרוּךְ אַתָּה יְיָ הַמַּחֲזִיר נְשָׁמוֹת לִפְגָרִים מֵתִים:

My God! The soul which You bestowed in me is pure; You created it, You formed it, You breathed it into me, and You preserve it within me. You will eventually take it from me, and restore it in me in the Time to Come. So long as the soul is within me, I offer thanks to You, Lord my God and God of my fathers, Lord of all works, Master of all souls. Blessed are You, Lord, Who restores souls to dead bodies.

(Morning Blessings in the Siddur, the Jewish prayer book)

It all started in the Garden of Eden,
a blissful place at the edge of the universe,
a wonderland oasis and paradise
planted by the Creator.

This Garden of God high above
is filled with blossoming groves of fruit trees
and watered by four roaring rivers
flowing from a common fountain at its center.

Right there, in the heart of the Garden,
is a majestic palace where God dwells
and which is guarded by a crew of archangels
carrying out His will as intermediaries with humanity.

It was an ordinary day in the Garden of Eden.
Archangels engaged in their usual tasks
in God's palace, while souls
enjoyed eternal rest
in the surrounding Garden,
taking shelter in its divine splendor.

"Go to the Garden of Eden," said God
to Archangel Michael, "and bring me a soul."
As he crossed the main gate into the Garden,
the Archangel encountered two souls
playing by the *Maayan*,
so called the central fountain in Hebrew.

"What's your name?" the Archangel asked
the first soul that came to greet him.
"My name is where you are," laughed the first soul.
"And what's your name?" turned the Archangel
to the second soul. "Also my name is where
you are," smiled the second soul.

The Archangel refused to accept their evasive answers.
"So, you both carry the same name?"
"Noooo!" giggled the two soulmates.
"I am Eden," announced the first one. "And I am Maayan,
the fountain that feeds the giant rivers of Eden," said the second.
"I thought Archangels were good with riddles."

"Don't be rude!" said Archangel Michael.
"You," he turned to Maayan, "stay here,
and you, Eden, come with me."
"Where do you take me?" inquired Eden.

"You have a meeting with God,"
replied the Archangel.
"Wow!" exclaimed Eden.
"Does God, Himself, wish to see me?"

"What an awesome opportunity
to meet the King of Kings.
Being in the presence of God
must be a startling experience."

But just the thought
of being alone In His presence
frightened Eden,
shocking and scaring her to move.

"I am not going anywhere without my friend, Maayan."
"Are you refusing to meet God?"
the Archangel raised his voice.
"No! I just want to go along with Maayan."

The Archangel looked at both of them
and said reluctantly, "OK, you can come together,
but I am not sure God will agree
to meet you both."

The two souls arrived at the royal palace
and bowed to the Holy One. "What's going on?"
God turned to the Archangel,
"I asked for one soul, not two."

"I chose Eden,
but she insisted on coming with
her buddy, Maayan,"
replied the Archangel shamefully.

"Is it true?" asked God. "Yes!" Both Eden and Maayan exclaimed in unison. "We always like to be together," said Eden. "Isn't friendship a quality the Holy One would like to find in everyone?" inquired Maayan.

"Dear souls," said God,
"I have a mission for one of you."
"A mission?" Eden and Maayan looked bewildered.
They thought only angels had missions.

"Yes, we're ready," they spoke loudly. "Well, maybe
I can send you both, if you insist, but each of your
missions is going to be slightly different," God proclaimed.
Eden and Maayan were delighted.

"What's the mission?" they asked.
"Going to Planet Earth," God announced.
"Earth???" shouted Eden and Maayan.
From what they'd heard, Earth was a dark and heavy place.

"Why would you take a pure soul like me,
emanated from You, the Supernal Light,
and exile it to this uninviting underworld?" asked Eden.
"Why can't you send us on a different mission?" questioned Maayan.

"Your mission is a noble one – to bring light
to that dark place," declared God. "How do we do that?"
"You will receive instructions," said God,
"There will be time for that."

"What is 'time'?" asked Maayan. God sighed.
"It is very hard to explain,
but while on a mission on Earth, you'll get it."
"Whatever you say," moaned Eden.

"You will also receive what you need to help you
complete your mission," God continued.
"It will be hard to understand at first,
but you'll have plenty of time to get used to it."

"Your Honor talks again about time," complained Eden.
"All right," God confessed. "The point is, I am giving you
something unique for your mission on Earth;
It is called a body."

"Thank you. But what is a 'body'?" asked Eden.
"You are impatient," responded God.
"I guess there's no point asking more questions.
We'll find out shortly."

"Wait, I have only one question," announced Maayan.
"What do you mean, we each have a slightly different mission?"
"You will have the opportunity to start together," God responded,
"But your mission will change when the time comes."

"Again you talk about time! I better stop asking
more questions," said Maayan disappointedly.
"That's right," said God. "Remember, the main thing is
to trust and not fear."

In a flash, Eden and Maayan found themselves
in a strange place.
They seemed to be in a kind of
a cave, smooth and soft all around.

The energy was dense,
but they moved through it easily.
They felt warmth, almost like being in the presence of God.
"God, where are you?" They shouted.

Then another Archangel, called Uriel, suddenly appeared.
He lit a candle and placed it on Maayan's head.
He then explained, "You are both
inhabiting a body that will gradually grow."

"You, Eden, will soon enter into the human world
as a tiny member of the human species.
You, Maayan, will be her hidden guardian
shining her way in this dark world."

Eden and Maayan listened carefully
to Archangel Uriel,
and this time they were fully
attentive without saying a word.

It was the first time
that they began to understand
the wondrous purpose of human existence
and the special roles they were going to play.

The Archangel also gave instructions
explaining how Eden –
through Maayan – could stay connected with
the higher world she left behind.

The general knowledge
that they could always stay together was exciting.
They were both radiant with joy,
feeling a glow of happiness.

They now understood what 'time' meant in the human world.
For a short time, they will grow together inside a human body.
Thereafter, Eden will leave and start
a new life in the human world on Planet Earth.

Maayan, on the other hand, will be
her guardian angel holding the candlelight of wisdom
for her and protecting her through
her entire life's journey on Earth.

Nobody among the humans will
ever know about this magic bond.
It is a secret
to be shared only by Eden and Maayan.

Archangel Uriel gazed sweetly at the two soulmates,
kissed them on their upper lips,
just below the nose, and before they could speak,
he disappeared.

Warm darkness surrounded them,
and they slipped into a deep, restful sleep.
When Eden woke up, she realized that her body
was going through a change.

She wondered what was happening,
and tried to remember what the angel had said.
There was something about beginning a mission,
assigned by God to carry out in my life.
I fully trust God's mission on Planet Earth.
But what were the instructions the angel had given?
.
Eden suddenly felt her memory clouded with fog.
She panicked and wanted to escape.
But then she heard an inner voice speaking:
"Remember what God said, the main thing is to trust, not fear."
"Oh, here you are?" She felt Maayan's body
floating near her and even touching her.

Many days have passed. Eden and Maayan
learned how to play together
as they were colliding
against each other inside the thick body liquid.
They even succeeded in holding hands
and kissing with their noses.

Sometimes, they were punching and kicking
each other like two boxers, and
never stopped their play-fighting.
But they spent most of the time
huddling together with their limbs intertwined,
interacting lovingly as two close sisters.

One day, Eden sensed something unusual
happening to Maayan. She did not move.
Her legs stopped kicking.
There was too much pressure from outside.
"What's going on?" She cried.
A moment later, Eden felt her body being touched and removed.

She felt her buttocks hit and liquid
pouring out of her mouth. She sensed a delicious
breath of life. She woke up crying. For the first time,
she heard a sound that came from her own tiny body.
She was scared. "Oh, my God, what a mission You
have chosen for me!" she was thinking.

Suddenly, Eden felt someone holding and rocking
her with a gentle motion. Feeling secure, she opened
her eyes and began to see shades of faces.
She then heard a sweet voice nearby
and sent a loving look to the eyes that gazed back with a smile.

It was her mother. "This is my mother!" She realized
and responded with a smile.
Apparently, it is part of the mission.
The loving voice and the tender touch reminded Eden
of the warmth and love of the world she left behind.

Recognizing Maayan's energy around her,
Eden knew deep inside
that a great miracle had just occurred.
She felt as if she'd arrived back home
to the delightful Garden of Eden.

When Eden grew up and became a big girl,
she explained to her cousins and friends:
"Everyone is born with a special mission.
But we forget what it is.
So how do we recognize our mission?"

"The little dent in the center above the upper lip,"
she pointed to the vertical groove below her nose,
"is a sign that a heavenly angel pressed on our face
to remind us that we always need to inquire and discover our mission,
so that life on Earth will be lived with a purpose."

The ultimate goal is living a purposeful and meaningful life.
If your purpose has not yet been fulfilled,
then your life has not been fully lived.
Regardless of your age, you have work to do
So you can be the best you can be.

Epilogue

Feeling common symptoms of stillbirth—no fetal movement and kicks of one baby—Natalie, the pregnant mother of Eden and Maayan, was rushed on December 8, 2002, to emergency care in Advocate Lutheran General Hospital in Park Ridge, Illinois. There, the physician friend, Dr. Haim Elrad, determined that Maayan passed away, and her surviving twin, Eden, must be given birth immediately. Both twin sisters were only 31 1/2 weeks old, weighing 3 lbs., 13.7 oz., and measuring 15 inches long. Maayan was buried in Westlawn Cemetery in Chicago, attended by the bereaved father, David, and grandfather, author Shai, as well as Rabbi Isaac Wolf.

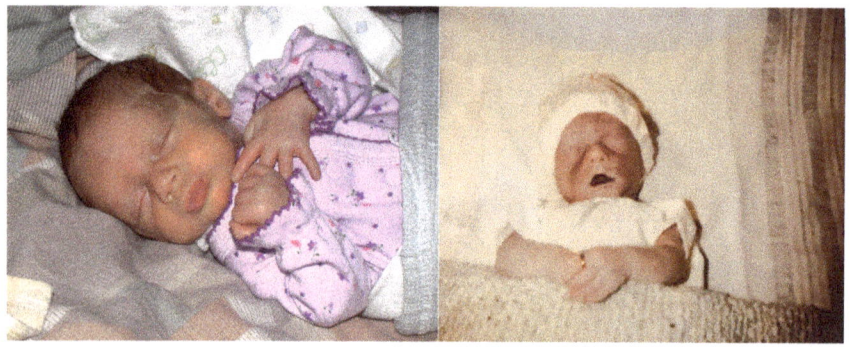

Baby born Eden   Stillborn Maayan

Maayan's Tombstone

Eden Visits Maayan's Tombstone in 2018

All cousins joining Liam's Bar Mitzvah in 2012

הִנֵּה נַחֲלַת יְהֹוָה בָּנִים שָׂכָר פְּרִי הַבָּטֶן:
כְּחִצִּים בְּיַד־גִּבּוֹר כֵּן בְּנֵי הַנְּעוּרִים:
אַשְׁרֵי הַגֶּבֶר אֲשֶׁר מִלֵּא אֶת־אַשְׁפָּתוֹ מֵהֶם:

Behold, children are a heritage from the LORD,
offspring a reward from Him.
Like arrows in the hands of a warrior
are the children of one's youth.
Blessed is the man whose quiver is full of them.
(Psalms 127:3-5)

אֶשְׁתְּךָ ׀ כְּגֶפֶן פֹּרִיָּה בְּיַרְכְּתֵי בֵיתֶךָ
בָּנֶיךָ כִּשְׁתִלֵי זֵיתִים סָבִיב לְשֻׁלְחָנֶךָ:

Your wife will be like a fruitful vine
within your house;
your children will be like olive shoots
around your table.
(Psalm 128:3)

About the Author

Dr. Shai Har-El is a historian, writer, poet, educator, rabbi, activist, and businessman. He was born in Israel, where he spent his formative childhood and young adulthood.

Har-El has been a successful financial professional and business owner since 1981, running his Illinois-based, financial services firm, Har-El Financial Group (see *www.HarelFinancial.com*). He was inducted in 1995 into the Hall of Fame of his parent company, Equitable, a national leader in financial protection strategies and wealth management (see *www.Equitable.com*), and has received many distinguished awards, most recently the Golden Year Award for achieving 30 years of high-level performance within the company.

Har-El is a founder and president of the nonprofit, ambitious, global nongovernmental diplomacy organization, Middle East Peace Network (MEPN) (see *www.MEPNetwork.org*). This organization uses private diplomacy to build bridges of understanding and reconciliation across the Arab-Israeli and the Jewish-Muslim conflict divides through human interaction, dialogue, education, and facilitation of peacemaking projects. He also gives lectures and workshops, and writes essays on Middle East affairs.

Har-El earned his B.A. and M.A. degrees in Middle Eastern History from Tel Aviv University, and his Ph.D. from the

University of Chicago, where he was recently appointed as a fellow at the Center for Middle Eastern Studies (visit *https://cmes.uchicago.edu/content/associate-members*).

Har-El is the author of the following history textbooks: *Struggle for Domination in the Middle East: The Ottoman-Mamluk War, 1485-1491* (Leiden: E.J. Brill, 1995); *Where Islam and Judaism Join Together: A Perspective on Reconciliation* (New York: Palgrave McMillan, 2014); and *In Search for Israeli-Palestinian Peace: An Urgent Call for a New Approach to Middle East Peace* (New York: Palgrave Macmillan, 2016). His last two books are the fruits of his peace advocacy and activism under MEPN.

Har-El was ordained as a rabbi in 2012. He has been running workshops and writing on a variety of religious themes, particularly on the interface between Jewish spirituality and personal growth. His forthcoming spiritual self-help book, *Discover the Jewel of Wisdom: Eight Paths to Powerful Living*, is a "living laboratory" report of his own personal findings while plowing the "fields" of life and his spiritual journey toward rabbinic ordination. His anthology, *Many Ways to Courting God: Selected Spiritual Writings*, and daily meditation guide, *Daily Spiritual Affirmations for Powerful Living*, were assembled as companion books.

Har-El's recently published poetry book, *Riding the Waves of Bliss: Seasons of Life Poems* (Grants Pass, OR: Homestead Lighthouse Press, 2020) is an insight into the changing seasons of his Life.

Har-El has lived for 40 years in Highland Park, Illinois, with his beloved wife, Rosalie of blessed memory, the central figure in his life for over 50 years. Their three children live in the U.S.

and Israel, with eleven grandchildren ranging from thirteen to twenty-four years old. This book is dedicated to them.

Contact the author directly at *shaiharel@comcast.net*.

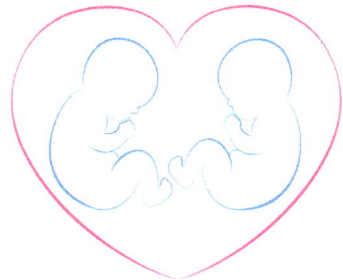

www.ingramcontent.com/pod-product-compliance
Lightning Source LLC
Chambersburg PA
CBHW041327110526
44592CB00021B/2843